T0392313

To order additional copies of this book, contact:
Xlibris
1-888-795-4274
www.Xlibris.com
Orders@Xlibris.com

ISBN: Softcover   978-1-7960-5529-0
        EBook   978-1-7960-5528-3

Print information available on the last page

Rev. date: 09/04/2019

All of America,
Israel, New Zealand,
Spain shall be
saved and half of
thee Netherlands.

Elijah Alexander

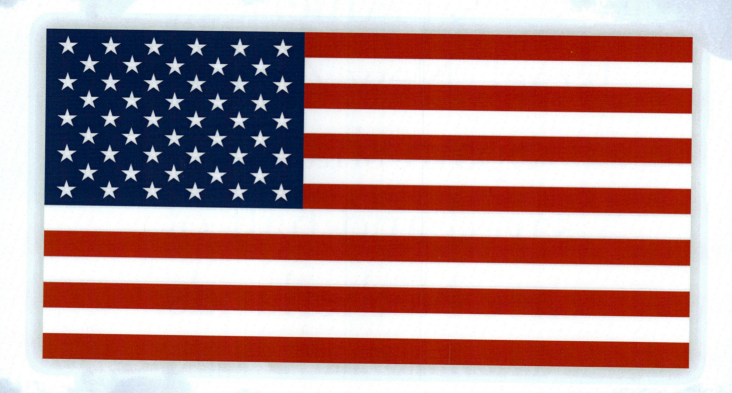

To: America thou hast made many mistakes but thou shalt overcome.

The Lord would say unto thee Thou Art kind & compassionate but lackest many things.

Thou needest to be certain about your salvation, where does it ly at. There is only one savior but thou servest many. Save a few. So now thou hast a chance to repent so repent, & now thou hast a chance to be saved, so be saved. There is great treasure to those who are saved. Doing bad things causes bad things to happen, doing good things causes good things to happen.

Over coming evil for good will cause a nation to be saved. Japan will be saved by this. & all the world can be too. Overcoming evil for good should be taught in our schools and if done in our schools they will become perfect. So therefore thou art called to. All of America can & will be saved by this. Amen.

To: Israel Rejoice Israel for thou shalt be saved, shake thyself & come to realize the facts whether good or bad there is deliverance from pain in it. There is soon coming deliverance for Israel. The Savior is coming back to Israel soon. He is your defense now & then. There is leading & guidance in every situation from the Lord. Back slide no more saith the Lord & great things will happen. Thou hast caused shame among the nations. But still thou art the greatest among all nations. For thou art a valiant people. There are many nations but not like yours. Thou art a week nation but thou shalt become strong. For the Lord of Hosts would say unto thee I'm the soon coming king I would say unto thee overcome evil with good & thou shalt be saved. All of Japan shall be saved by this & you will to. For the Lord of Hosts would say unto thee congratulations Israel thou shalt be saved & it is important to stay saved. The battle is not over when thou art saved. For the Lord of Hosts would say unto thee for this book nations can be saved by it. & it will be a great help.

For the Lord of Hosts would say unto thee.
I am the soon coming king so rejoice.
For the Lord of Hosts would say unto thee
Rejoice & be prepared to join God's Army.
For the Lord of Hosts would say unto thee
Trust & believe & thou shalt succeed.
For the Lord of Hosts would say unto thee
All Israelites shall be saved both Jew & Gentile.
For the Lord of Hosts would say unto thee.
I am the Savoir & there is no other.
For the Lord of Hosts would say unto thee

Focus on the Lord & his sayings, & thou shalt be rich.

For the Lord of Hosts would say unto thee

Be a doer of this book & the world shall be saved.

For the Lord of Hosts would say unto thee

For this book is not as great as the Bible but one tittle difference at present time.

For the Lord of Hosts would say unto thee.

Jesus wept for thee & his works still works today.

For the Lord of Hosts would say unto thee

For if David was alive today he would say serve him & not me.

For the Lord of Hosts would say unto thee Rejoice & be blessed.

To: New Zealand All of New Zealand shall be won by this book.

Trust & obey & thou shalt be saved.
Overcoming evil with good works if there's a positive flow thou shalt be saved.

For the Lord of Hosts would say unto thee

Congratulations thou shalt be a changed nation.

For the Lord of Hosts would say unto thee

Do you want to be strong serve the Lord.

For the Lord of Hosts would say unto thee be courageous & not fearful, the Lord does not delight in fearfulness.

For the Lord of Hosts would say unto thee

Smile for God loves thee.

For the Lord of Hosts would say unto thee

Correction works so be corrected & thou shalt be saved.

For the Lord of Hosts would say unto thee.

Be delivered from foolishness.

For the Lord of Hosts would say unto thee

Put the Bible first & this book 2nd.

For the Lord of Hosts would say unto thee

If thou shalt serve me thou shalt blossom forth into a beautiful nation.

For the Lord of Hosts would say unto thee

Separate thyself from carnal sins.
For the Lord of Hosts would say unto thee.
Come join that marriage supper of the lamb.
For the Lord of Hosts would say unto thee.
This book is equal to the book of Proverbs.
For the Lord of Hosts would say unto
Thee true wisdom is found in the Bible.
For the Lord of Hosts would say unto thee carnality destroys.
For the Lord of Hosts would say unto thee.
As a whole bless Israel & thou shalt be blessed as a whole.
For the Lord of Hosts would say unto thee
For there is a Army of the Lord join it.
For the Lord of Hosts would say unto thee.
There shall be showers of blessings on thee this day & forth.
For the Lord of Hosts would say unto thee
Depart from sexual sins it destroys thee.
For the Lord of Host would say unto thee.
Correct thyself & you shall be saved if not you won't.

For the Lord of Hosts would say unto thee.
If you dance, dance only in the Lord.
For the Lord of Hosts would say unto thee
Be baptized according to Acts 2:38
For the Lord of Hosts would say unto thee
Correct judgement comes from the Lord.
For the Lord of Hosts would say unto thee
If thou art a new comer do the simple things in the Lord such as read Bible,
pray, go to church & give such things as you have.
For the Lord of Hosts would say unto thee
Creating denominations doesn't work so don't do it.
For the Lord of Hosts would say unto thee
Speak evil of no man.

For the Lord of Hosts would say unto thee
If it takes little by little to get saved do it.
For the Lord of Hosts would say unto thee
& when thou gettest saved reach out to other nations to be saved.
For the Lord of Hosts would say unto thee.
Love heals.
For the Lord of Hosts would say unto thee
New Zealand you have the chance to win the heart of God.

To: Spain. Someone is coming to you & that is the Lord, & all of you shall be saved.

Overcoming evil with good works try it. Here are a few examples, mowing neighbor's yard, giving someone that is sick a ride to the doctor, sharing clothes with someone in need.

For the Lord of Hosts would say unto thee.

All Spain shall come out of trouble if thou shalt do these things.

For the Lord of Hosts would say unto thee

Look for the Savoir.

For the Lord of Hosts would say unto thee

Check yourself & see if thou art saved if not apply this book to yourself.

For the Lord of Hosts would say unto thee

Change not & thou shalt not be changed, change & ye shall be changed.

For the Lord of Hosts would say unto thee. For I am not ashamed of thee so do not be ashamed of me.

For the Lord of Hosts would say unto thee.

For there is proof in you that Christ lives so keep it & march on.

For the Lord of Hosts would say unto thee.

Trust & be good & thou shalt be saved.

For the Lord of Hosts would say unto thee. For there is a law & that is mankind
& there is another law from God, which one will you choose.
For the Lord of Hosts would say unto thee.
Be ye kind & generous towards one another in a Godly way.
For the Lord of Hosts would say unto thee.
For you are special & kind many preachers shall rise from thee.
For the Lord of Hosts would say unto thee.
Come & I will make you fishers of men.
For the Lord of Hosts would say unto thee.
Sworm thee earth with the gospel.

For the Lord of Hosts would say unto thee.

When thou art all saved reach out to the world.

For the Lord of Hosts would say unto thee Be soldiers for Christ & overcome.

For the Lord of Hosts would say unto thee.

Overcoming evil with good works.

For the Lord of Hosts would say unto thee.
Dream big & greater you get there by.
For the Lord of Hosts would say unto thee.
Reach out & thou shalt be reached within.
For the Lord of Hosts would say unto thee
There's only one salvation & that's from God.
For the Lord of Hosts would say unto thee
Be special & be thyself.
For the Lord of Hosts would say unto thee
If you had a million dollars & a Bible which one would be the most important
to have? Thee Bible.

For the Lord of Hosts would say unto thee.
Jesus is coming soon what are you going to do about it?
For the Lord of Hosts would say unto thee
There's only one salvation & that's from God.
For the Lord of Hosts would say unto thee
Be supportive of Israel & thou shalt be blessed.
For the Lord of Hosts would say unto thee
Strengthen thyself in the Lord.
For the Lord of Hosts would say unto thee
All Spain shall be saved & more.

For the Lord of Hosts would say unto thee.
As a newborn do the simple things in Christ Read Bible, Go to church, Pay tithes overcome evil with good.
For the Lord of Hosts would say unto thee
Love the Lord with all your heart, soul mind & strength.
For the Lord of Hosts would say unto thee.
After thou art saved you have the potential to save the world.
For the Lord of Hosts would say unto thee
Congratulations you shall be saved.

To: The Netherlands.

Ask & thou shalt be saved, overcome evil with good. Bless Israel & thou shalt be blessed. The good shepherd is Jesus Christ & he will do you no harm. Comfort ye another with these words. Satan is a deception so don't follow him. Jesus is real follow him. It thou shalt be saved nations will be saved. Be not afraid to support Israel you can pray for them, send missionaries to them & in doing so you can care for them & share Jesus with them & many other things. Jesus is coming soon so watch for him. Your favorite song should be I surrender all. After you are saved let God empower you. Love the Lord & he will love you back greater. Jesus is not a whimp but thee opposite. Jesus is the reason for everything. Christ is coming back & he wants you to be saved. Jesus weeps for thee cares for thee & loves thee & whisheth thee no wrong & there's no reason to be against Christ. Trust in the Lord & he will never fail thee. So dream big & let big things happen. Why think small there's no use for smallness. Do not get caught up in holidays that are not good. Do not get caught up in wrong sports. Do not get caught up in Rock-N-Roll, do not get caught up in sin & the Lord shall love thee. Jesus is that Blessed redeemer & there is no other. One half of the Netherlands shall be saved by this book but that doesn't mean the rest can't be saved. Amen. So be saved by other means. Amen. If you serve the Lord God will meet all your needs financial, food, clothing housing. etc.

Strengthen the Brethren even if they belong to another country for we are all brethren if were saved. Amen. Bless your Pastor for he is your shepherd, pray for him, support him financially & every little thing you can. Do not get caught up in new sins but rather do away with them. Get rid of all sin in your country & ye shall be saved. Do not be shy about using Gods angels to help thee. Strengthen the brethren when they are weak. Ask not & thou shalt receive not, Ask in faith & ye shall receive & if your faith is great enough you can have it all. The Netherlands shall be saved by other nations & this book. Congratulations, after that reach out. There is no errors in this book so you can-go by it fully. For the Lord of Hosts would say unto thee go by it fully & teach good things about it to other nations. Fight not against each other for it weakens your nation, also stealing, divorce, killing etc. But if you join hand in hand & be good to each other you will grow greater & there is no limits in it. For the Lord of Hosts would say unto thee make sure every adult gets one of these books plus some minors. Read this book over & over & you will grow. So do you want to be strong follow after all Righteousness & you will. The Bible says where there is no vision the people perish so have a vision for Christ. Deliver thyself from unnecessary pain study it out & do so says the Lord. Trust not in uncertain riches but the word of God. Thou shalt all be saved if you trust. When thou shalt overcome ye shall overcome. God bless's the just & thee unjust But beware unjust is wrong & it comes to an end. There is a savior & his name is Jesus Christ and there is no other. God is for thee & not against thee. God wishith thee no harm. But if you do not obey you will be punished. God is not ready to beat you down if you sin. But there comes a time when ye shall be judged. Jesus is coming soon. But all Bible prophecy must come to pass first. What would you do standing in front of an angry God. Sorry to say but many will & it will be an horrible experience so therefore overcome evil with good. Have you ever been burned hell is just like that so we need to avoid it. All psychology is wrong so don't go by it, it will lead thee astray. So God would say to the Netherlands I wish thee no harm but if you don't obey you will be punished & there is no measure in it. God would say be happy, be strong & do the basic things in Christianity. Amen.

Printed in the United States
By Bookmasters